James Kilgore

Harvest House Publishers
Irvine, California
92714

LETTERS ON LIFE AND LOVE

Copyright © 1978 Harvest House Publishers
Irvine, California 92714

Library of Congress Catalog Card Number 77-84893
ISBN 0-89081-112-1

Printed in the United States of America.

DEDICATION

For Jan

A little sister, a mature woman, a friend

CONTENTS

Introduction

A letter holds a very private communication. Writing allows one to express thoughtfully his feelings for another person—especially when he has difficulty verbalizing those feelings face-to-face. These pages represent real life experiences I have had with women in a counseling office. Some are actual letters I have sent and been given permission to use in the book. Others I have created for this project, but always with a real person and situation in mind.

These letters are personal in tone. The intimacy shared by the therapist and his patient rivals the intimacy of the family. I do not treat lightly the confidence shared with me. Nor is the counsel offered by mail considered insignificant. I want to share these experiences with you because some of them may touch on areas of your own struggle. Perhaps some will reinforce your joys. Others may recall your sorrows or support your successes.

While in graduate school I did some research on the pastoral writing of John Calvin. Out of his personal suffering, the harshness of many of the theological rules in his system were softened in application to life circumstances. My theology as well as my psychology and philosophy will be revealed in these letters. I offer these insights partially as an expression of my struggle to apply the instruction of the "letters" of the New Testament to my life and work.

Finally, I write letters like these to people I like. And I especially like women! My life has been blessed with significant women—a mother, a grandmother, a sister, a daughter, and above all, an exceptional wife! To these I have added numerous meaningful encounters with female friends, associates, employees, and counselees. My favorite women appear in this book, and so do some of the most intriguing and unforgettable ones. To each of you, friend and teacher, I say "thank you."

Part One
Of Men And Marriage

"Loyalty, life love, creates its own image of what we see."

Charles Colson

1

When Can You
Really Be Sure Of Love?

"For love is blind, and lovers cannot see."

Shakespeare
Merchant of Venice

Dear Dr. Kilgore:

You may not remember me. I saw you several years ago when my second marriage had fallen apart. The divorce was finalized and I married Doug two years ago.

Today is our anniversary. I'm ashamed to say this but there isn't much spark left in our lives. I wonder if I love my husband. He says he loves me, but I just don't feel what I think I should.

How can I be sure of love? Friends tell me I'm

lucky to have a husband like Doug and not to worry about my feelings.

It is hard for me to really put my thoughts on paper. Perhaps there are no answers to my problem. I hate to bother you. I know you are awfully busy, but anything you could say to me might help.

Anxiously,
Sally

P.S. I saw your book, *Being a Man in a Woman's World* in a downtown store. I bought a copy for Doug. I want to read it too.

Dear Sally:

Deep within each of us is the desire to love, and the longing to be loved and accepted. This is your dream, but in three attempts at marriage that dream has been shattered. Each time you reached out hungrily for love it eluded you; it was always out there, but never became a warm, live part of your relationships. I recall in our conversations, I caught a glimpse of the intensity of your deepest feelings. Let me share some reflections about love with you.

What is love really? Certainly love isn't something that walks up to us in another person's body. Of course, we can be loved by others. When love happens in a lasting sense, we begin to see it first internally before it is expressed externally. We must learn to love and accept ourselves before we can accept love from another person. For only then, can we give away true affection and care.

Sally, what you long for most is to see a sparkle in Doug's eyes that says, "I want you." But you know that being sexually attractive to him just isn't enough. It's true that love in marriage is built on a strong sexual foundation, but without something more the relationship soon falls apart. Love is more than fast breathing and physical excitement.

When I was a boy, I visited a farm and watched while some trees were being pruned. I learned something about the process of grafting. It seems to me that a loving marriage is like two varieties of trees being grafted together. Each can produce good fruit independently, but when they are brought together through the uniting process, they now produce a new hybrid version of the fruit—a better quality than either of them could have previously produced. (I'm referring here to a quality of life, not to having children.)

When a man and woman love each other, that experience does not sap away their individuality or limit either of them. Actually, loving is caring so much for the other person that you are willing to allow freedom for growth in the life space that is his or hers. I recall a line that says, "At the heart of love there is a simple secret: the lover lets the beloved be free." Unfortunately, I think each of us has a tendency to see ourself as the object and not as the ONE doing the loving.

Love at its best and highest is an outgoing, affirming experience. It doesn't cost me anything because I give it away. All the receiver has to do is accept it.

Perhaps that's the most troubling memory of my conversation with you about your feelings of not being loved. You seem to be waiting for love to happen to you. When I fantasize what you have told me about yourself, the picture I see is of a candle waiting for someone to strike a match and light it. Then the candle will illuminate the room. You are like the candle, which is crying out, "Why doesn't someone light me so that I can illumine the room? I would make such a bright light."

However, when I view human relationships in what I think is a clearer perspective, being loved is more like a small flame or a glowing ember in the fireplace. The relationship is the bellows which gently blows on the flame that is there and intensifies it until it bursts into a more demanding and roaring fire. The bellows alone could not create a roaring fire. The flame must first be present. Your expectations may be too great for your husband. He cannot create love within you; he can only fan the flame and increase its passion as he expresses his feeling toward you. And you must do the same for him.

The secret of loving is in its direction. It is outgoing more than incoming. When I'm so busy caring about and reaching out to the one I love, I don't have time to worry about whether I am being loved. Concentrate on loving him deeply and richly; the result will be more than a surprise, it will be satisfying. What you can be sure of is your own love for another person. When you doubt that, there is no satisfactory reassurance of being loved. You don't "fall in love;" you jump in with both feet.

Happy Landing,
James E. Kilgore

2

At The End
Of The Rainbow

"In bed we laugh; in bed we cry;
And born in bed, in bed we die;
The near approach a bed may show
Of human bliss to human woe."

Isaac De Benserade

Dear Dr. K:

I felt so relieved when I left your office today.
I just had to write this note to you and leave it
with your secretary.

Someone else finally knows my painful secret
besides Roger. I have felt so alone because I
dared not talk to another woman. Not being
able to reach a sexual climax has created within
me a fear that I'm not really a woman—at least
not all that I *should* be. But Roger has known

that something was wrong with our sex life, even though it is painful for him to admit it. He really avoids discussing these things because he doesn't like conflict. I think he could be a better lover, but can he learn how to satisfy me?

Please help me find the answer to the riddle of my sexuality. I think I'm ready to face my problem now because of our first session. I don't even know what an orgasm is or how to have one. I have faith in you. I know you can help me.

Sincerely,
Marian

Dear Marian:

Congratulations! I want to celebrate the risk you took today in my office. It takes great courage to open the bandages and expose the scars of your soul. The tears you shed represented years of frustration and pain. I'm glad many of them are released now.

To be 36 years of age and to never have experienced the total sexual release called orgasm is a tragedy. Saying you are not alone or even blaming your husband for being a clumsy lover may both be true, but neither satisfies the curiosity of your body or the craving in your heart.

You asked me two different questions: What is an orgasm and how can I have one? I want to give you some straight answers.

An orgasm is a simple, yet complex, physical-emotional-spiritual process. At its physical level it is simply a build up of bodily tension to the point of release. For some women that release explodes with deep muscular spasms, tightening and thrashing of limbs and verbal gasps and groans. Other women physically experience a soft tingling throughout the body's system, like a pleasant response to warm water rippling over your body. There are thousands of variations in between those two extremes. Numerous books have been written by women which more adequately describe the physical sensations than I can.[1]

But what you want in your marital bed is more than physical. It is also emotional. There is a psychological satisfaction born within the psyches of two lovers at the moment of union. Intimacy is more than touching bodies. Eyes look beyond pupils to see into the well of love.

1. *Becoming Orgasmic: A Sexual Growth Program for Women* by Julis Heiman, Leslie Lo Piccolo and Joseph Lo Piccolo, Prentice-Hall, Inc. New Jersey, 1976 and *For Yourself: Fulfillment of Female Sexuality—A Guide to Orgasmic Response* by Lonnie Garfield Barbach, Ph.D., New American Library, New York, 1976.

Ears hear a music more sublime than a glorious orchestration. Oneness becomes a momentary reality. In that experience the anxiety of loneliness is diminished. One feels interest, concern and shared depth through the satisfying lovemaking experience.

The spiritual level is the rarest arena of human exchange in loving behavior; yet it is undeniably the height and depth of intimate interaction. Whatever a soul is, it is surely touched when two beings deeply tap into each other's inner chambers. Words are not needed but can enhance those hallowed moments. Prayer is sometimes a spontaneous response to the nearness two feel toward God when they are so close together. Man, woman and God become a triune reality.

That majestic experience begins with some very practical steps. I have been teaching, in male sexuality seminars, the four gifts that a man gives a woman in human loving: mind, mouth, hands, and penis.[2] I just want to emphasize the hands here. There are two touches by lovers; giving and taking touches. Your man can lead you to the threshold of delightful response by learning the art of gentle giving through touch.

2. *Being a Man in a Woman's World* by James E. Kilgore, (Irvine, Ca., 1975), Chap. 6.

You must learn that touch first before you can appreciate it from him.

Before you allow the bricks of fear to be laid into a wall of inhibition, try an experiment. After your bath, visually explore your body in a mirror. Then gently touch yourself, exploring your own body and accepting the pleasure of your own hands. When you have become comfortable with your own touch, it will be easier for you to guide your husband's hands, and to "teach" him to give you pleasure.

Human sexuality is like a fine art. There are two major dimensions in its pursuit: discipline and reflex. Knowledge and practice make up the discipline; uninhibited movement in ecstasy become the expression of reflex. When I took piano lessons, I had the "feel" for being an artist. I enjoyed performing, but I wasn't disciplined. Without that essential ingredient, I could never be an artist. The discipline of practice requires time and the commitment of energy. After one has repeatedly played an arpeggio for hours, he may perform it with a sense of flow. He no longer has to think of each detail and note for his practice moves have passed into the realm of fine art.

Using your body in satisfying sexual relationship is much the same. In your initial experiences, a good deal of the interaction

betwen the man and the woman is more like
discipline than reflex. One of the reasons I
believe in a monogomous marriage is because it
provides an ongoing context for this "practice"
of sexuality. When familiarity grows, comfort
and relaxation also increase, allowing for more
uninhibited exploration. This discipline will lead
to the ecstasy of reflex as you are patient with
each other.

Here there are two extremely significant
words I hope you and Roger will discuss
often—setting and trust. Few women ever
achieve their sexual zenith without them.

Setting is important. Privacy is a must for that
initial breakthrough. Fear of discovery only
speeds stimulation and excitement, it rarely
deepens the pleasure. It takes time to savor the
delights of lovemaking. I suggested to Roger
when we talked that one of the most important
gifts a man can give a woman in lovemaking is
an atmosphere of trust where she can fully let
herself go with him. Just the experiences of
planning these moments together and stealing
extra time from your busy schedules will
enhance your sexual pleasures. Taking the time
to talk openly about your feelings will enhance
your mutual trust.

Finally, let me suggest to you that it is
important for you to learn to ask for what you

want sexually. Don't be afraid to give guidance to your husband, both verbally and non-verbally, as you seek new dimensions of sexual pleasure. You've waited a long time, Marian; don't be afraid now to run the risk of asking for what you want. While you can see the rainbow, find the gold. Come out of your lonely and painful sexual isolation and begin to explore your own body. That first orgasm will be worth it. Like the magical end of the rainbow, one day—perhaps without expecting it—you'll be there. I wish you speedy satisfaction.

Cordially,
James E. Kilgore

3

Infertility Is Not Failure!

"O Lord of heaven, if you will look down upon my sorrow and answer my prayer and give me a son, then I will give him back to you, and he'll be yours for his entire lifetime."

Prayer of Hannah,
I Samuel 1:11, TLB

Dear Dr. Kilgore:

Today is one of those days when I feel so discouraged I could cry. Let me write my thoughts to you while I'm depressed. Maybe that will help you understand me better.

Randy and I have been trying for three years to get me pregnant. The gynecologist has us on a regimen he says will work. I'm getting to the place where I'm almost tired of being in bed. Sex is less satisfying and becoming more like a chore. These feelings are beginning to frighten me.

I see women in maternity clothes and I envy them. Why is God punishing me when I love children so much?

I'm even beginning to question Randy's love for me. But I know he wants a child, but sperm on demand is less than exciting.

Help me, please—all of this hurts.

Sincerely,
Marilyn

Dear Marilyn:

Pregnancy happens so easily for some women and yet it can be such a struggle for others. It is so terribly disappointing to try so hard and have nothing happen. Sometimes I think we "try" too hard. And right now, you and Randy are feeling the loss of spontaneous sexual pleasure as you wrestle with the "chore" of getting pregnant. You are not alone; this is quite a common experience. Since no single solution exists, look at some additional options. Consider artificial insemination; think about adoption. These methods have been used satisfactorily by other couples to satisfy their desire for children.

I'm sure of one thing; God isn't punishing you by withholding a child. The Old Testament is filled with *human* explanations about why God functions the way He does. We can identify some of our pain with these explanations, but we must not limit God by human ideas about Him. While problems of life are frequently unexplainable from our perspective, I like the attitude of the little boy who looked up at the sky one night and said to his parents, "It must really be beautiful from God's side!"

For the present I suggest that you and Randy take a vacation from the "pregnancy problem." For the next three months, put away the thermometers and the charts. Plan fun weekends at the mountains or the seashore. Rediscover each other and enjoy being together. Spend time talking to each other about your deepest feelings on life as well as what having a child means to you.

Randy may have as many fears as you do about infertility. He could be questioning his manhood. Undoubtedly he experiences strong feelings of inadequacy and may be tortured by a sense of failure. He may wonder if a child will affect the way you treat him. Now he has your loving energies all to himself. When the baby comes he will have to share your attention and that can be a rather threatening thought. As anxiety rises, so does the tension level. Pleasure is reduced and the resulting frustration limits sexual satisfaction. The results can effect both of you and undoubtedly reduce the chances of successful conception.

I do want to caution you about one thing. The worst thing in the world is for you to think irrationally about your goal. If by chance you should not become pregnant, your life is not meaningless. Do you remember the feeling you had when you thought you would "die" if a certain boy didn't ask you to the prom? Or how "horrible" it would be if you couldn't get a new dress for that special occasion? Sometimes we react that way to more important life goals. But remember, you are still a very special and gifted person. Randy has told me how much he loves you. I do hope you have a child. You would make a wonderful mother. But if it doesn't happen, your world won't end. Your exceptional qualities will serve you well in other relationships.

I think of the place of influence you have as a nurse. So few people have your sensitive touch. I know that some of your caring needs, even some "mothering" functions, are fulfilled in the hospital room. Your patients are very fortunate people! Your sympathetic care and empathetic understanding contribute to much healing about which you may never know. But above all, you're every inch a woman, and I hope my letter comes along as one of life's "warm fuzzies" for you today.

Sincerely,
James E. Kilgore

P.S. I came across this quote I thought you would appreciate now, "Tears are often a telescope through which distant dreams are brought closer and made a reality."

4

Forgiveness Is Expensive

"Forgiveness to the injured does belong
for they never pardon, who have done
the wrong."

John Dryden

Dear Dr. Kilgore:

I'll get right to the point. I have lost faith in
Dick. "We" declared bankruptcy last week and I
am absolutely humiliated.

I am particularly disturbed about losing the
money I loaned him from my savings account. I
worked five years and wanted to use that money
for a down payment on a house. I may never be
able to forgive him for hurting me like this.

What can I do? Our family has never had a
divorce, and I hate to kick him when he's down,
but I feel like leaving.

I'm not very good in a crisis. I hope writing

you and whatever you write back will help me to clear up my thinking. I just don't know what I should do.

Desperate,
Mary

Dear Mary:

Do you remember those words, "To err is human; to forgive is divine?" Dick's humanity is certainly showing, and I pray that your "divinity" will show, too.

When you told me Dick had declared bankruptcy in the business and had also lost the money you had planned for the down payment on your house, I could almost feel the bitterness in your voice. I can only imagine how you feel—betrayed, disappointed and, yes, grieving over the "loss" of your anticipated new house.

I recall the sparkle in your eye when you told me you were pregnant. And your joy as you planned to buy the house could not be mistaken—you were like a kid with a new toy. I can almost see you now, crying because that toy is hopelessly broken.

A shattered dream is difficult to restore. To forgive Dick's "blunders" in business is going to be expensive. How can you do that?

As I write you this letter I think back to the

time in my life when I failed miserably. The faith that another person had in me meant a great deal in restoring my own confidence and hope for the future. I want to express my faith in you today. I hope it will be equally as helpful as you search for a new perspective.

Crises often bring people closer together. This financial disaster may reunite you and Dick in a sense of need for each other. It seems strange how one's values are immediately focused in a time of stress. Your most severe loss now may be your faith in your husband.

The conclusion of that beautiful passage on love in the Bible concludes with these words: "There are three things that remain—faith, hope, and love; but the greatest of these is love. Let it be your greatest aim." [1]

Your most significant question now is, "Why do you love Dick?" If your answer is because he provides financial security, then your relationship will be virtually destroyed by the bankruptcy action. If you love him for other reasons—which I'm sure is the case—this loss will hurt, but will eventually become only a painful memory woven into the fabric of your lives together. The vow to share life "for better

1. I Cor. 13:13-14:1, TLB.

or for worse" takes on new meaning when the "for worse" experiences occur.

It takes great courage and faith for a woman to go to her husband when he has failed and reassure him of her love. It's risky to try to forgive someone who doesn't ask for it. Such an expensive life energy as forgiveness sometimes must be held until it is requested. The heart ready to forgive, however, is the one ready for full living. The person too small for forgiveness cannot feel the magnitude of life's blessings.

If forgiveness is expensive, then bitterness is debilitating. Don't allow the harboring of spiteful feelings to eat like a cancer at your inner strength. A fettered spirit results from concealed resentment. I hope you won't fall into that depressing state of mind.

Be patient with yourself and with Dick. Use today well for it is the first day of the rest of your life.

With faith in you,
James E. Kilgore

5

Pick Up The Pieces
Of Your Heart Gently!

"Groanings which cannot be uttered are
often prayers which cannot be refused."

C.H. Spurgeon

Dear Dr. Kilgore:

I simply cannot understand what is
happening to me. I have never had anything hit
me as hard as Hugh's "affair." Some days I wish
he had kept on lying and not told me the truth.
Other times I feel better because I know, but it
still hurts.

I have so many questions. How did I fail as a
wife? Men don't "run around" if there's good sex
at home. Isn't that true? I keep asking myself
how I could be so stupid. Why didn't I see what
was happening?

I guess I'll never understand what prompted

him to tell me about the other woman. How
he could ever justify being unfaithful in the first
place is beyond me.

How can I cope with this pain? I'm going
crazy. Help!

Brokenhearted,
Karen

Dear Karen:

Even the shattered fragments of a broken
dream need to be handled with care. Those
crushed remnants I saw when you told me about
your disappointment are your heart. Pick the
pieces up gently!

There is nothing that can adequately prepare
a woman to hear the news about her husband's
affair, especially when it comes from his own
lips. That shock rivals the news of the death of
the one you love; it tears at the fabric of your
being. Our minds struggle to block out
unpleasant or threatening signals. Your mind is
no exception. As you look back, the clues are
like neon messages blaring against the night's
darkness, but you couldn't or wouldn't see them
before.

"How could I be so stupid?" "What are our
friends thinking? Who knows and who doesn't
know?" "I can't face our social obligations

unless I know what others have heard." Are those the mocking questions and accusations flooding your brain now? I know them only because some other bruised egos have screamed their pain into my ears before you.

Too much reflection can be psychological murder! The result of being rejected feels a lot like lifelessness. The common symptoms are depression, numbness, and those awful crying outbursts that strike seemingly without warning. The closer and more intimate the relationship with another person, the more powerful and devastating is the reaction to rejection.

You have attended some boxing matches with your husband on business trips. Have you ever seen a knockout? The punch that puts the man down for the count is usually a short, quick jab made from a close physical distance. Long windmill-like swings are rarely effective, even though they are exciting. Rejection by a mate is like a knockout punch; it hurts more because it lands so quickly and comes from someone so close.

Karen, don't rush to judgment—either of yourself or of your husband. Give yourself some time before you make any decision. Your feelings have already started to change.

You need to consider all of your options both

with Hugh and without him. A decision has been forced on you by his actions. Your challenge now is being realistic instead of vindictive. Indignation in the face of a predicament adds little judgment value. The resources you need to face this are there deep within you.

Decide your destiny on the basis of who you are, not on what someone else does. Whatever Hugh did is his own responsibility. Playing martyr will not enhance your chances of reconciliation. Nor will the lofty, self-righteous role coalesce the elements of your shattered intimacy again. Act on your love, using your good reason. Move calmly toward a decision you will be able to live with for years to come. Impulsivity undoubtedly tripped Hugh; don't trigger the same trap for yourself. Express your feelings fully and listen carefully to his responses.

There is no justification for marital infidelity. Consequently, a confession can only be met by a spirit of forgiveness or by an acknowledgement that the relationship is irreparably damaged. The only right I hope you'll keep in sight is the right of your freedom to decide what you want. If you cannot forgive Hugh, you'll never be free of that vengeful attitude. If you do forgive him, from that freedom will grow the options for your future whether it is together or apart.

I'm beginning to sound like this advice will be easy to follow. Believe me, I know that right now you want more than anything else to find a dark corner in which to hide and to never have to face any of these decisions. The pain you have experienced is brutal. I don't in any way underestimate the awful impact this has had on your spirit. Remember, however, that a pearl is the result of an oyster's response to pain. That irritating grain of sand or intrusion into the inner life of the oyster grows into something very priceless and precious. It can also be true for you and me. How we handle the intrusions into our hearts very often measures our personal pricelessness. Deal gently with yourself; the sun will rise tomorrow.

Reassuringly yours,
James E. Kilgore

6

Facing Separation Hurts

"God's most insistent call to us will always seem
a sort of silence, since his language isn't what we
expect."

Evely

Dear Dr. Kilgore:

When Frank came home this weekend, he told
me he thought we should separate for a while.
You had told me this was likely to happen, and I
thought I was ready. But now I'm not sure.

Can anything good come of his not being with
me? Isn't separation *always* a step toward
divorce? I fear that Frank will learn to enjoy
living away from me. Perhaps I will even
like having him in his apartment and will adjust
too well to our being apart.

I'm just not so sure that we will accomplish the right things. I'm too mixed up. I feel relieved when he's gone and tense while he's home, but I'm afraid to lose Frank.

Panicky,
Joanne

Dear Joanne:

Separation is always a painful experience. For many it is like surgery without benefit of anesthesia. One's emotional flesh is torn apart, and the heart is unceremoniously ripped from its protective safety within the chest cavity. The love flow it once pushed with each pulse can rarely be sustained.

Emotional pain results from most separations, especially those like yours, where the husband wants "out" and you want to stay "in" an ongoing marriage. Rejection is psychological murder in an intimate relationship. Fortunately, most lovers have more lives than cats to sustain them through these kinds of experiences.

Before you see your world falling apart, sit down with your husband and talk together about what this separation means to each of you. I've found that these actions generally fall into three categories: negative, neutral, and positive separations.

The *negative* use of separation is when it is a substitute for divorce. Husbands or wives who cannot be honest enough with their spouse and acknowledge that they want the marriage to end, often take what appears to be a more appropriate step—separation. These partners assume that after a period of separation, the other mate will join them in feeling that the separation is going to be good for both of them. I have rarely seen it work that way. The spouse who does not really want a separation, but is forced or manipulated into that position, often feels more anger and hostility later, when the separation can be clearly seen as a step toward divorce.

I am not suggesting to you that all separations that eventually end in divorce begin as negative separations. Sometimes they began in other ways, but end up being negative because they actually were ways of hiding feelings from each other, rather than a means to clarify these feelings. Substituting separation for a more specific and appropriate action such as divorce usually brings negative results in the lives of the couples with whom I have counseled.

Another way of using separation can be called *neutral*. In this case, neither of the partners can honestly say that they want a divorce, but both feel a loss of love and integrity in their relationship. The period of separation is intended to be a time to reevaluate and experience each other in a different setting so as to discover what stimulations to their love or assurances to their doubts can be found in the process. Neutral separation is a gamble; one never knows what the results of the separation will be.

A third kind of separation is what may be described as *positive.* In this case, both partners in the marriage believe that they have deep and abiding feelings for each other, but that experiences and problems in their lives have formed a wedge between them. The separation is intended to allow the unimportant obstacles between them to be worked out or dissolved so that their stronger and more pervading feelings can emerge at the center of the relationship.

Primitive farmers used the wind as a way of separating the good grain from the less desirable and non-nutritional huskings. This "chaff" would be blown away from the grain when the farmer tossed it into the air and only the good grain would fall to the ground. For some couples, separation is like tossing your marriage into the air and allowing the unnecessary appendages and non-nurturing problems to be blown away by the stress of reality. This can be a very positive move for a couple.

Joanne, I am not trying to explain away the pain of a separation. But I do want to help you find a rational way to deal with your situation with Frank. I would suggest to you that any separation arrangement be structured by a clear understanding in advance. It is important for you two to talk about what the separation means and what you hope to accomplish in the separation experience.

Separations built on haste usually result in increased anger and greater divisions between the couple. But a separation can be a more positive and helpful experience if both of you will agree on its purpose, your own guidelines for your behavior during the separation, and a way of evaluating its success or failure at the end of a specified time. Being a good salesman, your husband will know that not only planning your work, but working your plan is essential to success. This is true in all human relationships; the more we recognize what our goals are, the better we can evaluate whether or not we have achieved them.

To be separated is difficult and often lonely, but it need not be totally debilitating and rob you of the joy of life. Life is a journey not a destination; I hope you will learn something about yourself on this "detour" toward your dreams.

Supportively,
James E. Kilgore

Part Two

Of Doubts And Decisions

"We know accurately only when we know little; with knowledge doubt increases."

Goethe

"I respect faith, but doubt is what gets you an education."

Wilson Mizner

7

"To Work Or Not To Work—
That Is The Question!"

"The hapless woman n'er can say, 'My work is done,' till Judgment Day."

St. John Honeywood

Dear Dr. Kilgore:

I heard you speak at my church last Sunday. I found your talk so fascinating that I'm writing to you about a problem Tom and I have right now.

Will our marriage be better if I don't work? We want to have children, but until then, Tom wants me to do "woman's work"—which to him means household chores.

I am not a women's liberationist, but I don't

like to think of a life of boredom. I want to have a challenge each day and housework just doesn't make it for me. I want to do what is right for me, but I don't want to hurt our relationship.

Can you help us with this dilemma?

Gratefully,
Betty

Dear Betty:

To work or not to work—that's a dilemma for many of today's women. Few free choices exist. A survey in 1976 showed that money is the main reason that wives work. Families with working wives have about 26%, or approximately $5,000 a year, more money than those with non-working wives. Cold cash can be pretty convincing.

I would suggest that you and Tom attempt to determine what kind of family structure you really want. Important to your discussion is the motivation for choosing your life-style. *Traditional* roles demand that the husband be a "breadwinner," and the wife be the "homemaker." There is nothing sacred about those divisions of labor, but they have produced successful marriages for numerous couples. Liberators, male and female, decry these roles.

Their only advantage would seem to be the possibility that a person might experience some other choices.

You may prefer a *transitional* life-style—one in which the traditional roles are temporarily or experimentally changed. The phenomena of the "house husband" is a result of this kind of experimentation. Early in many marriages a wife earns most of the money while the husband finishes school. When I was graduated from college, the wives of all seniors received an honorary P.H.T. degree (Put Hubby Through!) at a luncheon prior to the commencement exercises!

There are some dangers for working wives—not unlike the feelings of many working husbands. The feeling of being taken for granted is one common complaint. Another resentment centers around the question of who has control of the wages earned. Who has the "say so" about where the money is to be spent? Many family arguments have ensued from this issue.

I have written a book called *Getting More Family Out of Your Dollar*, where I discussed fully most of these issues. One point I made is that money is a symbol of power and all power must be negotiated. In democracies, votes are the delegators of power. In the family, similar agreements should be reached. No *assumed* power is trusted. Husbands and wives, as well as children, need to talk out their expectations and evaluate their decisions regularly.

Try using these three guidelines for your potential decisions: One, gather accurate information; two, evaluate the facts in the light of your goals; and three, make a decision in your best interests as they are reflected in your relationship. If you have some choices, think about these factors too. If your work schedule has you working at different times, you will relax, eat and often sleep on independent schedules. Every *marriage* needs time together—to share ideas, meals, sexual pleasure and recreational play. If your working schedule and that which Tom follows separates you too much, whatever the values of working, the destructive influence on the relationship may not be worth it. *Don't* sacrifice permanent values in the face of an immediate crisis.

Working on similar schedules can produce the spirit of cooperation in sharing chores, transportation schedules, and planning how to use time off together. One young husband and wife took a picnic lunch once a week and met at a downtown park, enhancing their moments shared at midday.

Working for your own fulfillment is the most satisfying reason to work. *If* your job is what you *want* to do and brings you emotional as well as financial return, you'll be a good worker. The happiest people in the work force are those who know what they enjoy doing and have discovered a way to be paid to do it.

Finally, Betty, don't sell housework short. I learned many years ago to ask women in my office, "Do you work *outside* the home?" Every *woman* who cares about her relationship works inside the home. She must! Her home, far more than for most husbands, is an expression of how she sees herself. Choosing to make your home a full-time expression of yourself can be like the commitment of an artist to a canvas or a writer to creative expression. There are few careers that can bring the kind of emotional and life fulfilling satisfactions that being a happy homemaker brings.

Somewhere in a book about the pioneering days of the West is this line describing a man's wife: "She set her foot on the sod and the wilderness became a home." I believe the art of homemaking is the finest of the arts—and the most demandingly complex. Certainly a woman will not succeed in the art of homemaking simply because she is biologically female. To believe that kind of chauvinistic nonsense is irrational. Yet, those women who are intrigued by the homemaking art reflect exceptional capabilities which rival the success a woman enjoys in any other chosen career.

The important thing is to be your whole person. Let your career within and outside your home be a splendid reflection of the talents and abilities that distinguish you. Then, your work will be enhanced by your total womanhood! Bon voyage!

Sincerely,
James E. Kilgore

8

When The Flame
Of Faith Dies

"I believe in the sun,
  even when it is not shining,
I believe in love,
  even when I am alone,
I believe in God,
  even when He is silent."

Dear Jim:

I dropped this note by your office to thank
you for having lunch with me yesterday.

I've been aware of being "away" from God so
long. I used to feel close to Him, but all I sense
now is distance. It's too bad you can't touch
God. I think if I could just reach out physically
and put my hand on "God," I would have fewer
doubts and fears.

I wonder if God has feelings like I do. Can he
sense my loneliness?

I don't like to think of God as father. My dad was so helpless when I needed him. Please pray for me. Somehow I think that you might help me rediscover my *lost* faith.

Thank you,
Sarah

Dear Sarah:

I enjoyed our conversation over lunch yesterday. Some of your questions and comments are still circling in my mind, not quite ready for a landing.

Discovery and renewal are processes made different only by time. The first blush of insight is often exhilarating and relieving. A renewal, later, of that insight is a return to the freshness and now familiarity of those feelings. Faith in God can be so complex. And yet it seems at times, that it is genuinely indescribable. "Lost faith" is also an experience not unique to you.

I have found my faith in God through people all my life. In a sense, when I lose touch with special people, I sense some distance in my relationship with God. For many, the opposite is true—losing people forces them toward "God"—but not for me.

If I am estranged from others, I am troubled in my feelings about God, too. I think this pushes me to examine the incarnation—a theological word describing the process of Christmas—when God "became" human.

So many of the descriptions of God, which are called anthropomorphism, are feminine as well as masculine in tone. That is particularly true in the Old Testament where one of the names for God in Hebrew can be translated, "the breasted one." It describes the succoring quality of the relationship God has with us.

Would you dare to think of God as your mother? In the early days of your life, her breast was your sole source of nourishment. Breast feeding provides more than natural food in important life sustaining energies. It gives the child an intimate, warm contact with her mother's body, reminding her that her needs are fulfilled in her life. Mothers never "run out" when we need them. There is a sense of security built in that feeding process. I think that closeness and dependence early in life is similar to the confidence and assurance a newborn "Christian" feels. He has discovered a new and boundless sense of dependability.

As the infant grows and leaves the breast, so the believer's relation to God changes with maturity. He leaves the necessary and sustaining milk of the dependency phase and grows into a more independent but dependable process.

The child "leaves" the mother but is never *not* her child. The newness of faith changes into a quality of living.

Unfortunately, quality must be tested. There's the rub! Purity is determined by fire in precious metals. Substitutes for quality fail the test. Strength prevails. The character in a woman's faith is shown in the lonely moments of her life. Those are the tests by fire.

Early in my life I learned that the absence of joy did not mean the absence of God. That is a hard tenet to hold. It was for Jesus, too. In his loneliest hour, he screamed in pain, "Why have You forsaken me, God?" God's seeming remoteness is in contrast to his *parental* role when we pray "Our Father . . ."

Your consternation over not having an *answer* to life's immediate problems reminds me of that Old Testament sufferer named Job. Your consolation may be as his was—the end of the test found him richer and multiplied far beyond his beginnings. Yet his early impatience and demands on God for explanations seemed to meet with a deaf deity.

Let me share an amusing incident another mother told me. As she turned the lights out in her young daughter's room, the child said, "Mommie, I'm frightened, I don't want to be by myself." The mother comforted her and said,

"Honey, you're never alone; God is always with you." "I know that, Mommie," the little girl protested, "But when I'm afraid, I want a God who has 'skin on' to be with me!" The little girl spoke for you and me didn't she? God would be a lot easier to understand, to feel, and to experience if He had "skin on."

Reaching out to touch God would be reassuring. Yet in a sense I can touch Him through special people around me and, more important, I can be touched by Him through them. Reach out and touch someone when you're alone—you may find God where you did not expect to discover Him.

I'll be praying with you that during the "drought season" in your life, you may learn in an even more exciting and more meaningful way, the recovery of your sense of intimacy with God.

Faithfully yours,
James E. Kilgore

9

How Do You Fill
A Hole In Your Life?

The Human Touch

'Tis the human touch in this world that counts,
    The touch of your hand and mine;
Which means far more to the fainting heart
    Than shelter and bread and wine;
For shelter is gone when night is o'er,
    And bread lasts only a day,
But the touch of the hand and the sound of
  the voice
    Sing on in the soul alway.

Spencer Michael Free

Dear Dr. Kilgore:

Thank you so much for taking time to come to the funeral yesterday. I really appreciated your presence.

I feel so lost without Harold, but I'm trying to be brave. I want to come to see you sometime. I need to talk to someone about the feelings I'm having.

It is already hard for me to be a widow. I guess I should be thankful that he isn't suffering anymore. At least, when he was sick, I knew what I was supposed to be doing for him. I can't seem to figure out what I should do with me now.

I've been a wife for over twenty years. I feel resentful that when Harold died I seemed to lose my identity. I know I ought not to feel this way. How can I feel differently?

Gratefully,
Rachel

Dear Rachel:

When I walked away from the graveside, I could see your tear-stained cheeks looking up; and I kept hearing those words, "How do you fill a hole in your life?"

Grief is a devastating emotion. In many ways it is like having a "hole" shot through your very existence. Pain is part of the initial reaction, mixed with a sense of loss and a stunned feeling of unbelief. After the first shock settles, guilt often follows; then anger. Finally, reality shames us out of our self-pity into a new course of action.

A suggestion for filling the void in your life is to start by experiencing *good* grief. Don't deny yourself the right to feel anything, whatever it is. Feelings in themselves are neither good nor bad; behavior alone can be judged, our feelings simply exist.

The first temptation is to block the feelings you might think offensive to your own judgment and the opinions of others. It is irrational to believe that we can avoid our unacceptable feelings and self-responsibilities. Whatever we deny and attempt to *store* in our inner being unfortunately erupts at unpredictable moments in our life cyle. So go ahead and grieve—get all your feelings out.

Be honest with yourself. Your feelings and thoughts won't all make sense. You feel relieved that Harold isn't suffering anymore; yet you are angry at being alone to face the rest of your life. Some days you will feel remorse for things you wish you'd have said near his death. Other days you will discover a note he wrote you or a gift that recalls a special time of joy you two shared. The loneliness then will seem overbearing.

But don't fall into the trap of self-pity. Feeling sorry for yourself is wasted energy—you don't appreciate your sympathy, and no one else is around to commend you for it. Carl Sandburg once said, "Life is like an onion; you peel one layer at a time, and sometimes you weep." Tears are disconcerting at times, but they assure us we are neither painless nor dead. Weep when you must, but not for the benefit of others.

If you will deal honestly with yourself, you can be trusted by others. You will also risk sharing your pain and joy with them. The void in your life will be filled with other relationships—not necessarily with a single male, but with people whose lives and love you can share.

Did you ever see the cement truck with the motto: "Find a hole and fill it!" A bit of a pun but the statement contains the truth. Out of the opening to pain in our own lives, we can often communicate understanding to others. The hole in your life may become a pouring spout for the needs of others in the future. The void you feel may in reality become a means of channeling your resources and transmitting them to others.

Grieve well and then gather up your resources, and get back into the giving game of life. The only love we ever really keep is the love we give away.

Hopefully,.
James E. Kilgore

Part Three

Of Pain And Pleasure

"Pain and Pleasure, like light and darkness, succeed each other."

Laurence Sterne

10

The New Secretary
Isn't Your Problem!

"A woman of honor should not suspect another of things she would not do herself."

Marguerite De Valois

Dear Jim:

We've known each other a long time. I've got a problem. I need some help, and I don't know where to turn.

George has hired a new secretary, Amanda—She's 22 and beautiful! She wears tight clothes, sometimes without a bra—and she is well-endowed.

How can I compete with a girl half my age? The body isn't what it used to be. Should I have

to tolerate her flaunting herself in front of him?
Maybe *you* could call George and set him
straight.

I've never felt jealous before around George's
office. But this new "Miss American" makes my
skin crawl. How can I convince him to get rid of
her?

Frustrated and fuming,
Carol

P.S. Don't tell me not to be jealous. I've already
tried that—the first two months. Go visit his
office and see "Miss Mini-Skirt" yourself! That
will convince you that the competition is unfair.

Dear Carol:

Jealousy is a cancer to a loving spirit. Left to
destroy the other life giving energies, one's
resentful suspicions can consume and infiltrate
until a depression as lifeless as death results.

Carol, I'm afraid you are infected with that
spiteful problem. I wish it were as simple as a
new secretary. Can I hold up a mirror for you
when you speak about her? Your words sound
so catty!

You can be sure of one thing. All men,
including your husband, will view a secretary
differently than you do. He may see her as an

attractive young woman half *your* age, but she is also *half* his age. Her interest in the job may include pleasing him and gaining his approval. She may, however, have very different feelings away from work.

Let me share with you three lessons that every jealous woman should learn. The first is that jealousy reveals more about the owner than it does about its object of focus. When suspicious and resentful thoughts absorb you, the secretary is not hurt! She doesn't get indigestion or have a migraine headache; you do. Your jealousy destroys you, not her.

The mirror, mirror on the wall doesn't say you are the smartest of all. Not on this point. Your friends may agree about how terrible it is in your presence, but they will wonder more about you than about George when that jealous rage bubbles over into the luncheon conversation.

The second lesson is that attempts to punish your husband when he doesn't feel guilty only create distance between the two of you. Trying to "protect" George from her doesn't draw him to you; it pushes him away. If she is a poor secretary, don't give him an excuse to keep her on the job because he doesn't want to feel "henpecked." If she is a good secretary, she shouldn't be penalized for her personal attractiveness. The more you "punish" George by withdrawing from him the more negative he will feel toward you, *not* her. Criticizing her is a subtle criticism of George's judgment. Few things can cool a man's passionate energies like feeling as though he has been "scolded" by his mother.

If your criticism of his choice in a secretary are correct, it will be harder for him to admit that to you if you have berated him about it. "I told you so" will only be a hollow victory. If you are wrong about the girl, you undermine his confidence in your judgment in the future. Don't let your jealousy lead you into either of these pitfalls in the future.

Finally, "reality test" your assumptions about the secretary. You may even learn to like her yourself! Encourage George to see her as you would want a boss to view your 22 year old daughter if she was his secretary. Get to know Amanda on a personal basis; she will be less frightening to you. When you can begin to see her as a somewhat nervous girl in her first full-time job, and then compare that to who you are and where you are in life, I think your jealousy will begin to look pretty foolish to you by comparison.

I can guarantee you, from my conversations

with George, that your 24 years of history together are a strong bond and not a millstone about his neck.

No real competition exists between you and George's secretary. She fulfills a different role in his life. Even if you were to consider her an "office wife"—one who can be supportive and understanding in his professional world as you are at home—there need be no sexual implication in the least within that relationship. Remember that the more pleasant his day is, the less likely you are to get negative carry over at home. A good secretary, with a good relationship to her boss, can be one of the greatest assets a wife can have.

A final caution—don't be so consumed in your jealousy that you *pretend* that you don't *need* George anymore. If you convince him of that, he may find it attractive to turn to someone who *does* need him, or he may simply withdraw inside himself as a way to handle the pain of your rejection. Either move on his part would tend to diminish the quality of your marital relationship rather than improve it.

Don't *assume* anything. On a diet of facts, jealousy withers into weakness. Half truths and fears nourish its growth. It is time for a new diet, Carol; don't let that jealousy bulge ruin your figure.

Yours for the freedom to be whole again,
James E. Kilgore

P.S. An Arabian Proverb reads: "Four things that are never brought back—the sped arrow, the time that has passed, the spoken word, and the lost opportunity." You aren't shooting arrows but your time and words could give you an opportunity to grow closer to your husband. Don't miss it!

11

The Beauty Of Your Body

"What is really beautiful needs no adorning. We do not grind down the pearl upon a polishing stone."

Sataka

Dear Dr. Kilgore:

I am writing you this letter because I'm not sure I can say this to you in person.

I'm an extremely modest person. I have great anxiety with my M.D. My husband complains when I have to undress in the bathroom. I always make sure it is dark before we have intercourse; all the lights must be off.

I've had these feelings since I was a little girl, and I'm now 35. I have two girls. I am trying not to inhibit them. I wish I knew what made me this way.

Can analysis or counseling help me with this?

Embarrassed,
Alice

Dear Alice:

Modesty is a virtue; the fear of nudity is not. The painful anxiety you have experienced about being undressed in front of your husband and your gynecologist is a concern which can be dealt with in therapy. It undoubtedly has inhibited the growth of your sexual relationship together.

You don't have to visit Sigmund Freud to do some analysis of your attitudes. Being in the nude is not sinful. If I read with understanding the story of the Garden of Eden, Adam and Eve were naked and unashamed before "sin" entered the world. Disobedience to God made them uncomfortable about their bodies. There is nothing inherently wicked about baring one's body.

Psychological risk is often so painful that we make it evil. I want to suggest to you that your fear of intimacy has focused on your body. Intimacy—of the soul or body—is fraught with danger. If I show you my "heart," you may disapprove of its content. You believe that if you show your body, the result will be rejection. Rejection, if it occurs, can hurt, but it is not evil.

More important than your comfort in a physician's office is the absence of tension in the privacy of your bedroom. And since I can't do much about the practice of most gynecologists, let me try to help you in the area where I can offer some suggestions, the relationship of your husband.

I am going to suggest something dangerous! Before you can be comfortable with anyone else viewing your body, you will need to be comfortable with yourself. I want you to look at yourself in the mirror, nude, and preferably in the daylight. What will happen is the beginning seed of appreciation for your body which the psalmist describes as "fearfully and wonderfully made." You may have to repeat this process a number of times before you begin to feel comfortable.

The second step will be to begin to share yourself with your husband. I know it is secure to get undressed and dressed in the bathroom and to have intercourse only in the dark and under the sheets. But your present behavior is habitual—conditioned by 35 years of thinking and acting in what "modesty" dictated. I believe you not only can but should change these patterns.

Start by admitting your own unhappiness and anxiety to your husband. Ask for his patience and support over the next three months. Beginning now you can be more comfortable within 90 days. Won't it be a new freedom not to have to hide your body?

Privacy and modesty are different. I don't expect you to be publicly exposed—your goal is more comfort in the private arenas of your life. Virginia Satir once wrote: "Because I own all of me, I can become intimately acquainted with me. By so doing I can love me and be friendly with me and all my parts. I can make it possible for all of me to work in my best interest." [1]

Take possession of your body and get to know it. Whatever anyone else may ever know can then be no surprise to you. Your purity is not in question; it is your comfort with yourself in normal life stress that is important.

Finally, your sense of "modesty" is the result of familial and parental conditioning more than any other single factor. I know that you will not

1. *Peoplemaking* by Virginia Satir, Science and Behavior Books, Palo Alta, CA, 1972, p. 28.

want your children, especially your daughters, to experience this kind of anxiety.

The loveliest of gifts that people may give us in the finest of wrappings are not useful unless we open them up. In opening the box we discover what the gift really is. In a similar manner, the greatest gift you can give your husband is the intimacy of your body, your soul and your spirit. Inhibiting actions in the physical realm also indicate a lack of openness in the psychological and spiritual realm. I urge you to begin now to open yourself up and share yourself as a step toward full relationship and development not only physically, but also psychologically and spiritually.

Hopefully,
James E. Kilgore

12

A Sword In Your Heart

"Hearts are stronger than swords."

Wendell Phillips

Dear Jim:

You've seen me through some real crises—a divorce, losing my job, the children leaving home, etc.

It's hard for me to say this. The wedding Susan and I had always talked about will never take place. She got married this weekend because she was four months pregnant! I don't know if I can ever forgive Donny. How could he do this to me?

I'm not sure Susan will have any kind of life with this boy. She says she loves him, and that they wanted to be married eventually anyway. But I don't see what she sees in him. I wonder if what I've tried to teach her all these years was wasted now.

Maybe I need to come to see you again. I feel so deeply hurt.

Painfully,
Pat

Dear Pat:

The words, "A sword shall pierce your heart," were first spoken to Mary, the mother of Jesus, by an old prophet near the temple in Jerusalem. How harsh and strange they must have sounded to her when she heard them at the time of the dedication of her son to God. Yet, every child has the possibility of cutting deeply into a mother's soul.

When I learned of your daughter's pregnancy, I remembered all the plans you had for her wedding. Losing your dreams must disappoint you. What concerns me most is your reaction to her choice of a husband. Stubbornness has led to many marriages, but conflicts between in-laws have to be "fed" to stay alive. Your new son-in-law does not have to be your enemy. If you force your daughter to choose between her new husband and you, the results will be bitterly disappointing. Only more pain for you and for your daughter will result.

No one knows better than you that youthful marriages brought on by premarital pregnancies are struggles at best. Is an 18 year old divorcee with a child a more attractive picture? Only to a mother whose need to be needed has blinded her view of other values.

At 36, you won't be in the Guiness Book of World Records as the youngest grandmother in history! But your daughter will need you as much as you needed your mother during your own pregnancy, first childbirth, and initial years of marriage. Whatever your wounded feelings, close the gap now and help her cope with this new and hopefully joyful experience in her own life.

People only change for two basic reasons: pain and potential pleasure. If this "shattered dream" of your daughter's future has created enough pain to give you new insight into yourself, she may have helped you more than hurt you. Not only can you potentially gain in your relationships to your younger children, you may also benefit in terms of other adults. Since your divorce, you've—as you put it—"run many men away." Perhaps your daughter's subtle rebellion against being controlled and possessed will also shed some light on how you relate to males.

Pain—"the sword in your heart"—can be a beneficient teacher as well as a demanding master. Use this experience well. As you face yourself in the mirror of life, don't forget the image you see. What you don't like, you can change, but only if you admit that it is present.

With God, no act on the stage of life is meaningless. I will be praying for you that *all* this may turn out for your ultimate good.

Empathetically,
James E. Kilgore

13

"Tomorrow Is A New Day"

"We know what we are, but know not what we may be."

Hamlet
Shakespeare

Dear Dr. K.

You will be surprised to hear from me. When I visited you last, I was a "working girl."

Guess what? I haven't turned a trick in six months! I am now working at—. I enjoy my job, and I'm learning to live on less.

I want to thank you because you were the first man who cared about me that I never slept with. As strange as it sounds, I'm kind of afraid of men now. I thought I could psyche out any man. Now I don't know. As soon as I told the guy I was dating about my past he wanted to go to bed. I refused to sleep with him, and I haven't seen him since that night.

Do you think anybody will ever accept me if they know what I did? Does God look down on me? I need to know.

I'll be waiting to hear from you. I trust you.

A new woman,
Michelle

Dear Michelle:

Your letter was a special reward for me. I was drawn immediately to my memory bank of experiences with you. Our first meeting is still a moment to ponder. When we talked about your "modeling" career, you said, "I am good at what I do." I wondered then why a prostitute would seek help from a marriage counselor. I confess you were initially a sensual oddity for me for I had never personally known a woman in your profession.

Your story intrigued me. I wanted to "explain" what made a farm girl turn call girl. Shortly, however, I reminded myself that you were a human being seeking acceptance. Looking back over those months when you revealed your soul visit by visit, I began to sense the changes taking place.

I am so proud of you! What a transformation has occurred. The *new* woman is marvelous most of all because of the genuine inner beauty. There is such a contrast to the past with its emphasis on outer beauty and the capabilities to seduce.

The past is a lingering problem for you, isn't it? Being careful about sharing that information is advisable. Not every employer or new "friend" can be trusted with the responsibility of that information. Ultimate judgment still belongs to God. He sees no difference between sexual immorality and pride or envy. People may seem to "look down" on you; God only "looks in" on your heart.

I wish you well on your new job. A place to work where you can find some sense of identity in what you do is very important. Finding your reward through hard work brings a special satisfaction. Employment may also open the doors to new friendships for you. Work on relating to women first; a nurturing respect between two females is important to you.

Fear of men seems like a strange feeling for you. Yet every form of escape is based on fear. Being unwilling to fail, the fear of rejection, and the anxiety over my reputation before others—each becomes a stone in the wall of separation and escape. You chose to escape through what appeared to be intimacy for years. Some choose alcohol or drugs. Others choose preoccupation with work. One can use almost anything as a place to hide from himself.

Finding a man to love is more difficult than sexual intercourse. He will want your body if he loves you, but not at the cost of your new treasure—your sense of integrity. When a man loves you, he will accept you for what you are, not for what you have been. His love will be based on his feelings now, not his views of your past.

Having learned to "psych" men out and do what pleases them, you now need to work on self-assertion. Asking for what you want is as important in a healthy marriage as giving what your beloved asks of you. Blaming destroys the other; placating reduces self-hood. Balance is the *delicate* art of relationships.

Michelle, tomorrow is a new day, and your life proves it. You're a living witness that being loved and accepted brings about a transformation.

Feeling a warm glow with you,
James E. Kilgore

14

How Do You Start All Over Again When You're 30?

"Revenge is sweeter than life itself. So think fools."

Juvenal

Dear Dr. K.

Several months ago I came to see you when my husband first started talking about how unhappy he was with our marriage. You may recall that he refused to come for an appointment.

He finally moved out, and we have just signed the divorce papers. He was as generous as my lawyer said he should be. I have enough money, but I don't seem to be coping too well with the emotional part of divorce.

When I got married, I thought it was for life. I didn't grow tired of Larry; he divorced me. What makes me mad is that his life goes on in the way he chooses. I'm stuck with the responsibilities of children and the house.

Life isn't fair to women, particularly a divorcee. How do you start over again when you're 30?

Angrily,
Elaine

Dear Elaine:

When I got your letter last week, I sensed the anger and hurt you were expressing. Your resentment of Larry's apparent "freedom" exploded off the page. I felt like writing you a "Time will heal the wounds" message. I decided instead to try to answer your question about reentry. Your query has lingered with me like a haunting melody that lightly teases the shadowy keyboard of the mind.

Being single again puts one back in touch with the anxieties of the premarital years. What do I say? How do I act? What is expected of me?

An inevitable reevaluation of one's self picture occurs during and following divorce.

Our psychological "defenses" are like the white cells in our blood forming a wall to protect us in crisis. In the body chemical changes are created, such as fever, to call attention to the danger. That's good! However, when the threat ends, the mobilization of certain body energy recedes.

Usually for a divorced person the psychological reactions do not return to rest. An irrational process sets in which is self-critical. To protect yourself from these negative feelings the easiest place to "unload" is against your ex-spouse. Afterwards, the feelings coalesce into loneliness or resentment. Neither result is pleasant.

"Starting over" certainly isn't easy. Perhaps the best place to begin is with a review of your assets and liabilities before and after your divorce. What really has changed?

Before the divorce you were already a mother and a proud homemaker. You worried then about the pressure of being a parent and a wife. The *security* of home ownership was already showing up as an energy consumer. Tension between you and Larry was almost always present.

After the divorce you have all of those treasure-troubles except a husband, with whom you had a bad relationship. I don't expect you to shout for joy when you read this. I know you are lonely and hurt. Some women believe a poor relationship with a husband is better than having no husband at all. I'm certain that isn't true. A Hebrew proverb says "It is better to eat soup with someone you love than steak with someone you hate."

When I wrote the "Divorcee's Bill of Rights," perhaps the idea which drew the most response was, "The Right to Live Without Remarriage if you Choose." Every person is *valuable* as an individual. Marriage neither adds to nor subtracts from your worth. It also follows that what you have succeeded in or failed at in a marriage relationship does not affect your value as an individual. There is a place to "start over" at any age—at the point of a new sense of your own worth!

When you feel differently about *who* you are, your perspective changes on *what* you do. Look in the mirror and see the person you are. When you look again at your children and your home, you can see how much they mean because you are *invested* in them.

A fresh start begins with a fresh look. I hope you see more than "left-overs" in the pantry of your life! I do!

For your bright future,
J.E.K.

P.S. Did you ever read this verse: "Two men looked through prison bars; one saw mud, the other stars." Look up, and live!

Part Four

Letters To Four Special Women

"There is no worse evil than a bad woman; and nothing has ever been produced better than a good one."

Euripedes

15

To Mom:
"Thank You for
Being a Christian!"

"Men are what their mothers made them."

Emerson

Dear Mom:

After 40 years of knowing each other, I thought it was time to reflect about what it means to be a son, particularly your son. Let me begin by saying "thank you" for some of the things that are very special about you.

Thank you for being intellectually curious. I am glad to be the son of a woman who did not check her brain in at the hospital in exchange for her baby. I am sure that one of the reasons that I am an insatiably curious person, a persistent reader, and an expressive writer is because you talked so much to me as a child. It is a joke that is still going on with your grandchildren that you are "generally speaking" around the house. That exposure to books and ideas, to people whom I could encounter openly and to educational opportunities is a priceless heritage. It has shaped much of my development as a person and as a parent.

Thank you, too, for not being possessive. You never really pulled the emotional umbilical cord. I'm sure it was difficult for you to see me traveling very early to other states or leaving home for a residence high school in the 8th grade. I know now that it was difficult to see me move all the way across the country when I married. The fact that you know how to let your children go became more evident when my sister went to South America. It is only when I think about my own children leaving home that I can appreciate the red eyes I saw the mornings we left home and the tears you so often shed in the airport. Thank you for enduring that pain and for not making me feel guilty when the urge to explore life found its wings in my experiences.

Thank you, too, for growing with me. It's hard to be a mother at 17. You must have struggled with that responsibility. You've always had a knack for using your resources well. One of those was your own parents. You gave me something very special by allowing me to experience their love and care when I was very young. While you could have tried to teach me everything, you were wise enough to use many people, including my grandparents to help shape me in the early days of my life. That was a wise choice for which I could never fully repay you.

Thank you for having an "open home," not only to your friends and mine, but to some truly great people who have influenced my life. It was always easy for me to invite my friends to come home for dinner or to spend the weekend. I never remember your saying that it would be too much trouble or that you were too tired, and I remember appreciatively having the kind of home where my friends were always welcome. The memory bank I have of meals we shared with visitors to our home is an immeasurable treasure. My interest in the world was sparked because of the missionaries from so many countries who told about their parts of the world around our dinner table. I have since learned that not only did they rub off on us, but somehow we shared a very special family life which seemed to be contagious to others.

Thank you for helping me to know what to

choose in a wife. Maybe I should really thank Dad for marrying you. You never sat down and said, "This is the kind of girl," but your ideas guided me as did the relationship you and Dad modeled. I somehow knew that a good marriage was made up of open exchanges, managing differences, and an ever present expression of care and concern. Above all, you have been a Christian mother. I don't want to excuse your frailties. You haven't always been right, but you have been *there* when the crises of life occurred. From the time you met Christ when I was 12, there was a difference in your life. It has become more visible over the years. I wrote this poem in 1963, but it still expresses many of my feelings about your sharing Christ with me:

MY MOTHER'S CHRIST
When I was but a little lad,
My Mother told me of Him

Who, though good, died for the bad.
She told me that He loved them.

And she would come and sit
By me and tell me of His fame.

I thought she was old fashioned
And that her Christ was too.

I could scarcely have imagined
That all of this was true.

I waited for the day to come
When I would be of age

And leave my mother's home
To star on this world's stage.

I would pay the winners price
For my mark on history's page.

But I met Him one day
In a quiet holy place.

There I knelt to pray
And claim His saving grace.

And through the years we walk
In perfect harmony

And through the day we talk
My Mother's Christ and me.

I often think where I might be
If Mother hadn't shared

The message of her Christ with me
And told me that HE cared.

Let me close this letter by thanking you for being a good grandmother. I've watched you with my children, your grandchildren, and have seen again many of those things that I experienced as a child. One Christmas, while we all sat around the tree opening presents, one of the special insights of that holy season suddenly reached out and grabbed me: God wanted His son to know what it was like to have a mother. Thank you for helping me to know what it is really like to have a mother.

Lovingly,
Jim

16

To Jan:
The Sounds Of Silence

(This an actual letter written to my sister
December 30, 1976 after the death of her eight
month old son.)

The Lost Voices

Northward again the happy birds, returning,
Shall sing for us the songs we thought were lost;
They were but waiting in a fairer country,
Untouched by storm and frost.

And when the lonely winter of our sorrow
Has rounded out for us Earth's changing year.
Oh, on some radiant morn what long-hushed
  voices
Shall greet our listening ear!

Annie Johnson Flint
(on May 30 "Short Pilgrimages")

Dear Jan:

Christmas Day may never be the same for either of us after 1976. A picture of you sitting in Northside Hospital with the lifeless body of James in your arms has burned itself into my brain.

He was such a pretty baby—aren't all uncles for whom nephews have been named allowed a special pride? I was thrilled when the news came from Ecuador that James (for me) Benjamin (Jacob's name for his last child by Rachel) Cabascango had been born March 31, 1976. My joy was even greater when you came "home" for the holidays to spend it with us here in Atlanta. Christmas Eve was so special for our family. I remember James' fascination with the fire. It seemed like hours he sat in my lap and watched the flames dance on the logs. In his beautiful baby wonder, he turned to me smiling and drooling, pulling at my ears and pressing those teething gums against my nose between gurgles. I'll always remember those moments.

Your babies have all been special to me. A big brother feels a responsibility for his only sister's children. When your first son, Timothy, died after only 7 days, I felt that unfinished agony across the miles from Los Angeles to Quito. Having visited Janet Victoria and John Phillip these last five years both in Ecuador and in Georgia, they feel almost like my own three. James was your last child, and I looked forward to enjoying "our Christmas" together with your James, my Jimmy, and proud Uncle Jim. I had a disquieted feeling when we finally finished preparing "Santa Claus" for the children and retired about 1:00 a.m. I had just gotten to sleep when I heard you rushing the baby to the car to go to the hospital. When I arrived moments later, we began that long vigil which ended with the physician's "I'm sorry; we did everything we could."

I have seen a side of you in the last few days which has made me proud of "my little sister." There is nothing small about your courageous heart and honest spirit. Through blinding tears and in the face of utter fatigue, I watched a woman cope with her tragedy. Each phase—from explaining to the other children that "James went to be with Jesus and Timmy," through the decisions about funeral arrangements—there has been an indomitable energy, touched with the softness of your femininity.

I know you will hear the sounds of silence, as

I do with you, for months to come. That tiny laugh, the gurgling smile, and that final scream just before death will compete for a place in your mind.

I struggled for a long time with these brief thoughts—mostly with passages from the Living Bible—when you asked me to have the services for James at the graveside. I am enclosing them with the letter.

I can't hurt *for* you in this loss, but my heart cries *with* you. Your life will never quite be the same—neither will mine. I hope my loving prayers will help you to begin to heal the wound.

Your brother,
Jim

P.S. These are the words I shared at the graveside.

A Moment of Worship at the Graveside of James Cabascango

December 27, 1976

We have gathered here at this grave today as a family to place into the ground the body of a special child—who lived less than a year, but whose life and death will affect us for years to come. We look to the Word of God for comfort as we face this moment, and we share with you our sorrow and our hope in the living Lord, and His Word.

"Be filled with the Spirit; speaking to yourselves in psalms and hymns and spiritual song singing and making melody in your heart to the Lord; Giving thanks always for ALL Things unto God the Father in the name of our Lord Jesus Christ.

"Rejoice with those that rejoice and weep with those that weep.

"And now, dear brothers, I want you to know what happens to a child of God when he dies so that when it happens, you will not be full of sorrow, as those who have no hope. For since we believe that Jesus died and then came back to life again, we can also believe that when Jesus returns, He will bring with Him all the Christians who have died . . . So comfort and encourage each other with this news.

"And once when parents were bringing their children to Jesus for Him to bless them, the disciples shooed them away, telling them not to bother Him. But when Jesus saw what was happening, He was very much displeased with His disciples and said to them, Let the children come to me, for the kingdom of God belongs to such as they. I tell you as seriously as I know how that anyone who refuses to come to God as a little child will never be allowed into His kingdom. Then He took the children into his arms and placed His hands on their heads and blessed them.

"He has filled me with bitterness, and given me a cup of deepest sorrows to drink . . . O Lord, all peace and prosperity have long since gone, for you have taken them away. I have forgotten what enjoyment is. All hope is gone; my strength has turned to tears, for the Lord has left me. Oh, remember the bitterness and suffering you have dealt to me! For I can never forget these awful days; always my soul shall live in utter shame.

"*Yet* there is one ray of hope; His compassion never ends. It is only the Lord's mercies that have kept us from complete destruction. Great is His faithfulness; His loving kindness begins afresh each day. My soul claims the Lord as my inheritance; therefore I will hope in Him. The Lord is wonderfully good to those who wait for Him, to those who seek for Him. It is good both to hope and wait quietly for the salvation of the Lord.

"And I heard a great voice out of heaven saying, The tabernacle of God is with men, and He shall dwell with them, and they shall be His people, and God himself shall be with them and be their God. And *God* shall wipe away all tears from their eyes; and there shall be *no more death*, neither sorrow, nor crying; neither shall there be any more pain; for the former things have passed away.

"And I say to you that you shall weep and lament, but the world shall rejoice; ye shall be sorrowful, but your sorrow shall be turned into joy. And you now have sorrow, but I will see you again, and you shall rejoice in your hearts and your *joy* no man taketh from you. And in that day you will not need to ask me any questions.

"It's like this: When I was a child, I spoke and thought and reasoned as a child does. But when I became a man, my thoughts grew far beyond those of my childhood, and now I have put away childish things. In the same way, we can see and understand only a little about God now, as if we were peering at His reflection in a poor mirror; but someday we are going to see Him in his completeness, face to face. Now all that I know is hazy and blurred, but then I will see everything clearly, just as clearly as God sees into my heart right now. There are these three things that remain—faith, hope and love, and the greatest of these is love.

"And now you have a new life. It was not passed on to you from your parents, for the life they gave you will fade away. This new life will last forever, for it comes from God. Our natural lives will fade as grass does when it becomes brown and dry. All our greatness is like a flower that droops and falls; but the Word of the Lord will last forever.

"Everyone dies because all of us are related to Adam, being members of his sinful race, and wherever there is sin, death results; but all who are related to Christ shall rise again.

"But someone may ask, How will the dead be brought back to life again? What kind of bodies will they have? What a foolish question. You will find the answer in your own garden! When you put a seed into the ground, it doesn't grow into a plant unless it dies as a seed first. When the green shoot comes out of the seed, it is very different from what you planted. You put in a dry little seed, and God gives it a beautiful new body—just the kind He wants it to have.

"In the same way, our earthly bodies which die and decay are different from the bodies we shall have when we come back to life again, for they will never die. The bodies we have now embarrass us for they become sick and die, but they will be full of glory when we come back to life again.

"These perishable bodies of ours are not the right kind to live forever. But I am telling you a wonderful secret: we shall not all die, but we shall all be given new bodies! When the last trumpet is blown from the sky, all the Christians who have died will suddenly become alive with new bodies that will live forever.

"When this happens, then the Scripture will come true—Death is swallowed up in victory. O death, where then is your victory?

"How we thank God for all of this, it is He who makes us victorious through Jesus Christ our Lord."

Let us pray: O God, our Father, we come this morning with broken and sorrowful hearts to this gravesite. You gave Cesar and Jan such a beautiful child—so happy and full of life. In a few short hours he made everyone around him smile and laugh at the wonder of life; you understand then, Lord, that we are struggling with the mystery and the pain that his death has brought us. It is so hard for us to rejoice in this thing, but we have heard Your word—we give thanks even in this which for us is a dark hour.

You did not spare your own Son, but gave Him at Christmas that we might not mistake the depth of your love. Jan and Cesar have lost a son. As your own heart was moved in the death of your Son, be moved in the death of this son—so precious to us. Pour out your love on our family; give us grace and peace in the hour of need.

Your Son lived only a few years on earth yet we are touched daily by His life. Their son has lived only a few months on earth; yet they will be touched for years to come by his life. So fill them with the beautiful memories so that the painful ones will be banished.

As you gave daily bread for food in the wilderness for Israel, but never more than a day at a time, give all who sorrow here strength for today and hope for tomorrow.

Through Jesus, Our Lord. Amen

Let me say a final word to all who listen to these words. Thank you for coming to share these moments of grief and sorrow. As a family we appreciate your concern, your thoughtfulness, and your presence.

We ask you to weep with us, but not without hope. We believe we will be reunited in Christ in the life that little James now knows. You have been with us here in our time of sadness; please make sure that Christ is the Lord of your life and join us there in the time of gladness too. If the death of this beautiful baby can be your invitation to be a child in the family of God, He will not have lived in vain.

Let us pray. The Lord bless you and keep you. The Lord make His fatherly concern shower upon you and give you peace. Amen.

James Benjamin Cabascango
March 31, 1976—December 25, 1976

17

To Joy:
"On Becoming A Teenager!"

"My son is my son till he have got him a wife,
But my daughter's my daughter all the days of
her life."

Thomas Fuller

Dear Joy:

When special occasions arise in a person's life,
it seems to me that a little time for reflection is in
order. Your special occasion for now is a
thirteenth birthday.

Thirteen years ago I stood in the hospital in
Pomona, California and breathed a prayer of
thanksgiving at your birth. For a few hours the
doctors had worried about the complications
that caused you to be born by the Caesarian

section method. Our *joy* at your birth so near the celebration of Jesus' birth made picking your name an easy assignment. Of course, the "Marie" is from your mother's name. Next to her, you are my special girl.

As you grew up, you were at times a joy—sometimes you were just very funny! You almost always had a cheery smile for everyone. That's a quality I hope you'll never lose. There's a glow about people who are sure of themselves that relaxes and refreshes those around them.

One of the happiest days of my life was the night in your bedroom in Athens when I listened as you asked Christ to be Lord of your life. And I was extremely proud to be able to baptize you that following Sunday night. There are some joys that fathers who are not ministers cannot share with their daughters.

Thirteen is a very special age. The teen years are fantastic, but they are also very problematic. You know how many parents come to me to talk about how to get along with their children.

You are on the road to physical adulthood and emotional maturity. At this point in your life, I want to ask you to help your mother and me to be the best parents we can be to you as a teenager. One of the things we will need is to have you talk to us about your feelings. Information questions are all right too, but talk to us about the things you want to share or the things about which you are not sure. We may not know answers to all problems, but we can listen because we love you. Those two things are very important in life—to be listened to and to be loved! We also need to have you listen to us at times, and we will always need your love.

I could get carried away with this letter, but I'll stop with a pledge to you. With your help, I'll try to be the best father I can be during your teen years. The world isn't what it was when I was your age; I'll try not to set back the clock! I love you very much. I want you to be as proud of me as your father as I am that you're my daughter.

Happy Birthday!
Daddy

18

To Ruth:

An Exceptional Wife

"If you can find a truly good wife,
She is worth more than precious gems!
. . . There are many fine women in the world,
but you are the best of them all!"

Proverbs 31:10, 29, TLB

My Dearest Ruth:

Letters are not new between us. I've been
writing to you for more than twenty years and
still haven't run out of words. Perhaps that's the
result of your "undefinable" quality.

Today, miles apart, I'm reflecting on my love
for you. I have been fortunate! Finding a woman
committed to being a wife is a rare discovery.
Living with you has brought rich delights.

From our first fumbling efforts on the honeymoon to our present comfortable sense of being a part of each other, I have tried to "know" you fully. The deepest intimacy of the Hebrew language is caught in the verb "to know." Yet I am aware that I incompletely comprehend you. What Gibran calls the "spaces in your loving" combine to make up the mystery of the unique elements called you.

Loving you has been to discover a child, eagerly playing, laughing, pretending, teasing, and enriching the humdrum with the excitement of your presence. Holidays and family gatherings have always been "fun" because you have refused to see any other possibilities. I think I was "born old;" you have helped me grow young.

Living with you has allowed me to watch the development of a person over two decades. What a beautiful woman you have become! I remember reading that if a woman is not beautiful at twenty, it is her parent's fault. If she is not beautiful at thirty, it is her husband's fault. If she is not beautiful at forty, it is her own fault! In your case there is no fault. The beauty of twenty has been enhanced by marriage and matured gracefully. Because you possess an inner faith in things that never age, neither do you.

Your special gifts in life are numerous, but not always obvious to others. When you perform musically, the public hears the quality of your voice and feels the joy you sing. Only those who have seen you on the home turf really know more of the real you.

What you are cannot be caught in words. You are reflected in a smile and a wave as the car leaves the drive . . . and the beauty of Spring in your plants . . . or the smell of something fresh from the oven . . . the dress made that morning . . . the ever present "I'd like to do that" to a neighbor's request . . . an "extra" helping in the school cafeteria line . . . special touches all over the house.

You excel with children. There are three full-bodied and well-adjusted teenagers who stand as testimony to your skills. Whether teaching them to cook or typing a term paper, you seem always accessible. No son or daughter ever lived who could be more fortunate than those three who call you "Mom."

I don't know what my life would have been without you. I'll always love you.

Your husband,
Jim

Conclusion

When confronted by criticism of the inscription he ordered for the cross of Jesus, the Roman ruler Pilate said, "What I have written I have written." I share his feeling in a much less dramatic way.

Few readers will agree with all of the advice or admonitions given in these letters. Some will be helped. You may be critical or curious. This "chapter" is my letter to you. I seriously invite you to respond to me when you have finished reading it.

As I gain perspective on my life, there are three insights which continue to survive in the constant swirl of idea assessment. The first and most pervasive idea of living is that intimacy and honesty are the greatest pleasures of existence.

To disclose myself to another person and to be accepted and responded to in an honest encounter is a priceless experience. One of the satisfying ways I remain psychologically in touch with some of my dearest friends is by personal correspondence—an exchange of love letters. What I have written here has been a sampling, shared with you and hopefully whetting your own appetite to write. I experience great curiosity when the mail is delivered, and find satisfying pleasure in producing correspondence that not only communicates but conveys caring.

A second living insight which energizes me is this: each day is a gift from God to be filled with productivity and learning. My pace in life is quickened by the myriad pleasures of people, experiences, and opportunities for exploration. What an exciting challenge to "soak up" the universe of personality! Or to plumb the depths of another's pain in the struggle of life. I regularly lie down with an exhausted satisfaction, even when I can't fit all of the pieces of the day's puzzle together. In no way would I imply that viewing life from this perspective is conflict free. My goals—short and long term—often collide with opposition. But I have discovered in the resolution of these conflicts a great reservoir of learning, both about myself and others.

Finally, learning that truth is the same in all arenas of life has helped me immensely. What is sound psychologically is also thoroughly true philosophically or theologically. If an idea will stand a sociological test, technology in the medical or educational fields it will verify it as well. Truth is verbal and non-verbal, complex and simple, but ultimately it must be tested personally.

When Pilate asked, "What is truth!?" he was looking at a man who said, "I am the way, the truth, and the life." Life and love have made more rational and emotional sense to me since I have discovered a personal relationship with Christ. Intimacy with God has meaning through him.

I hope these letters will serve as an invitation for you to read the greatest love letter ever written, the New Testament. Welcome to His world for more letters on life and love!

James E. Kilgore
P.O. Box 76684
Atlanta, Georgia   30328

Other Good Books
From Harvest House

BE THE WOMAN YOU WANT TO BE, Ruthe White.
Some women set out to resolve all their problems on their
knees, in scroungy bathrobes and unkempt hair. Others
seek to win their victories in the beauty shop, at the lingerie
counter or in a spa. Somewhere in between is a balance.
This book presents that balanced perspective that helps
you exercise your individual right to a rediscovery of
yourself. 1148—$2.95 (paper)

FOREVER MY LOVE, Margaret Hardisty, writes from a
woman's point of view of the husband's responsibility to
his wife, his family and his church. She explains the female
mind in a way that allows the husband to provide for the
emotional needs of his wife. This outspoken book,
appealing to husband and wife alike, is the first of its kind
for today's man. 0017—$2.95 (paper)

THE SPIRIT-CONTROLLED WOMAN, Beverly LaHaye
writes from a woman's point of view, giving the Christian
woman practical help in understanding herself and
weaknesses she encounters in her private life and in her
relationship with others. This book covers every stage of a
woman's life—teen dating, the single career woman,
motherhood, divorce, widowhood, menopause and others.
0206—$2.95 (paper)

YOU CAN WIN WITH LOVE. Out of a most disastrous
experience in broken relationships, God taught Dale
Galloway that His kind of love wins again and again.
Climbing from the deep valley of self-loathing and
loneliness to the heights of acceptance and love, he has
lived and *experienced* all that he writes about. 0249—$2.95
(paper)

MIX BUTTER WITH LOVE. A beautiful and practical cookbook written by Joyce Landorf—especially for her daugher-in-law. Inspirational—devotional—and full of delicious easy-to-prepare recipes for family and guests. A delightful gift for your daughter-in-law, your daughter or your special friend. A colorful, padded edition. Illustrated by famous artist, Francis Hook. 0354—$6.95 (gift edition)

A FAMILY LOVE STORY—the journal of a family in love with each other and with others—leads the reader through the joys and sorrows of a typical Christian family throughout its years, focusing especially on the children's trying teenage years. Lou Beardsley gives us a beautiful heartwarming guide for the Christian family. 0176—$2.95 (paper)

THE SENSITIVE WOMAN combines the secular and the spiritual in a refreshing approach to developing sensitivity. It gives guidelines to increase awareness of needs, drives and desires in oneself and hence toward others. By Sandra S. Chandler. 0370—$1.75 (mass paper)

HE TOUCHED ME. God touched one—after years of searching. He touched another—and conquered her pride. And another—while seething with hatred; and another—while in the valley of depression. In this beautiful book, Ted Miller compiles and edits the life-changing experiences of women of many and varied professional pursuits. 0095—$1.45 (mass paper)

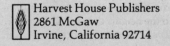

Harvest House Publishers
2861 McGaw
Irvine, California 92714